Herbaceous Perennials

GRAHAM RICE

D0492328

Cassell

The Royal Horticultural Society

THE ROYAL HORTICULTURAL SOCIETY

Cassell Educational Limited
Villiers House, 41/47 Strand,
London WC2N 5JE
for the Royal Horticultural Society

First published 1992
Reprinted 1994

British Library Cataloguing in Publication Data
A catalogue record for this book is available from the British Library

ISBN 0-304-32027-7

Photographs by Graham Rice, Harry Smith Collection and Michael Warren
Line drawings by Mike Shoebridge

Phototypesetting by Chapterhouse Ltd, Formby
Printed in Hong Kong by Wing King Tong Co. Ltd

Cover: this traditional herbaceous border at New College, Oxford, has a yellow and mauve theme.
   Photograph by Harry Smith Collection
Frontispiece: Papaver orientale 'Black and White' has attractive seedheads once the petals drop; it is best propagated from root cuttings (see p. 57).
Back cover: a group of mixed perennials and grasses, seen in late summer. Such a display should last well into autumn.
   Photographs by Michael Warren

Contents

Introduction

WHAT IS A HERBACEOUS PERENNIAL?

This is a question that often provokes lively discussion. The definition given in *The New RHS Dictionary of Gardening* is 'perennial plant which dies down to the ground annually', so more questions arise: Surely this includes bulbs? What about pinks and all the other 'herbaceous perennials' which are evergreen? Does it include bergenias, which are not only evergreen but also have stout woody stems? And how about fuchsias, undeniably shrubs but prone to behave as herbaceous perennials in many gardens?

Argument will doubtless continue, but for the purposes of this book we have to draw the line somewhere. And of course the solution must be both practical and pragmatic. So our line corresponds with that customarily drawn by gardeners – perhaps tentative but nevertheless clear.

It is not evading the issue to say that this book covers those plants which most people refer to as herbaceous perennials, and which feature in books and catalogues under that heading. This, of course, includes delphiniums, phlox and Michaelmas daisies, which die down completely every year. Hellebores are in, despite the fact some have stems or leaves which persist over the winter; so, too, are euphorbias. I do not include bulbs which clearly come in a well-defined category of their own. Neither do I admit fuchsias, phygelius or perovskias, which, although they may be cut down to the ground by frost or secateurs, are undoubtedly shrubs. Bergenias are clearly not shrubs, so they find a place here.

I realise that my approach may irritate purists, but this is a book for gardeners.

Part of the splendid herbaceous borders at Arley Hall, near Northwich, Cheshire

Where to Grow Perennials

There are two strands to the developing use of herbaceous plants in gardens. In herbaceous borders and island beds, perennials have exclusive right to the territory and indeed these features have been developed specifically to show off perennials to their best advantage. Yet herbaceous perennials have also been grown in cottage gardens where they have taken their chance with the fruit, the herbs and the chickens. And in mixed borders with a wide variety of other plants, the perennials often contribute to the success of the whole.

HERBACEOUS BORDERS

In large gardens herbaceous plants are traditionally grown in the herbaceous border, a formal planting usually backed by a wall or yew hedge. The plants are arranged in groups which are kept separate and not allowed to intermingle. Generally, the tallest are planted towards the back, grading to the shortest at the front. A border of this sort makes an impressive feature, especially as at Arley Hall and Newby Hall, where parallel borders are separated by a grass path. It is at its best in the summer months.

The annual maintenance of such a border consists of lifting, dividing and replanting perhaps one-third each year, digging and enriching the soil with organic matter at the same time. Plants are set out in groups of three, five or more depending on the size of the border. Between replantings, the border is given a dressing of general fertiliser each spring, and it may also be mulched. The hoe is used between the plants until their foliage meets and smothers any weeds. Staking is one of the most important jobs in such a border but it is time-consuming and can be an expensive business. The whole border is usually cut down in the autumn and the sections not due for replanting forked over lightly and left tidy.

At its peak such a border can be stunning, and immediately

Islands beds at Bressingham Gardens where the taller plants are grouped towards the centres of the irregularly-shaped beds

before and afterwards it can still look pretty good. In a garden large enough to accommodate other plants for other seasons the herbaceous border will undoubtedly appeal as an impressive way to feature perennials. In winter, however, it will be undeniably bleak, and planting too many spring and autumn flowering plants will detract from its impact in summer. Moreover, certain aspects of its maintenance are time-consuming, in particular the regular replanting and, as mentioned, staking.

ISLAND BEDS

The island bed is a concept developed by Alan Bloom of Bressingham Gardens as a way of displaying perennials without the necessity of a formal border set against a hedge or wall. Informal beds, often laid out in sweeping curves, are designed to be viewed from all sides. The size and shape of the beds are arranged according to the space available. They may be roughly oval or kidney-shaped but are not normally regular in outline.

The beds are planted with the taller varieties towards the centre. The plants grown are those which are self-supporting, generally those of naturally short growth, or shorter-growing varieties of naturally tall plants. The advantages of growing perennials in island beds are that such plantings can be fitted into gardens and situations not suitable for a traditional herbaceous border and that the use of dwarfer cultivars virtually eliminates the time-consuming task of staking.

COTTAGE GARDENS

In cottage gardens and in modern cottage-style plantings hardy perennials take their chance in the rough and tumble with all the other plants. Traditionally, plants which are easy to divide have long been cottage favourites, and this explains why in many villages you tend to see the same plant in almost every garden. The same goes for plants which self-sow easily. Either way, the perennials have had to hold their own with the shrubs, fruit, vegetables, herbs and sometimes poultry. Those that require pampering have tended to fade away, while the more invasive among them had chunks heaved from them and discarded. This accounts for the unlikely plants sometimes found in hedgerows near villages. So, with occasional human intervention, the cottage garden has settled into an uneasy equilibrium, with shade-loving plants finding homes either under the shrubs and fruit or under taller perennials.

THE MIXED BORDER

It could be argued that a mixed border is little more than a sophisticated version of a cottage garden. Small trees, evergreen and deciduous shrubs, climbers, hardy perennials, bulbs, some of the tougher alpines, annuals, biennials and bedding plants, plus ground-cover plants of all descriptions, are grown together in a carefully planned and thoughtfully maintained planting. It is in the mixed border that the art of associating plants is brought to perfection, so that the whole is more effective than the sum of its parts.

Hardy perennials play a crucial role in this increasingly popular approach to planting and will often be the most numerous plants. Popular because the mixed border can not only be adapted to any situation in a garden of any size but also because the use of so many other kinds of plants enables us to realise our aims more effectively. In particular, whereas an island bed or herbaceous border can be bare and featureless in winter, it would be hard to achieve the same result in a genuinely mixed border.

There are other ways of growing hardy perennials. A bed may sometimes be set aside for just one favourite – though it had better be a good one – or for a single group of plants like delphiniums or peonies. A few selected cultivars can be grown very effectively in meadows, while some are ideal for containers, either as single specimens or in mixed plantings.

A cottage garden where herbaceous perennials mingle with roses and annuals – all in delightful profusion

Colour Schemes and Plant Associations

Growing healthy plants should be the aim of all gardeners but if the plants are arranged badly, the garden will still be a disappointment. Learning to group plants together so that they enhance one another can take time and requires a discriminating eye. Looking at other well-planted gardens and taking note helps immeasurably.

The easiest way to create a colourful display is to choose plants which enjoy the same conditions and flower at the same time, and then to plant them all in a single border. Colourful, yes, but satisfying?

There are a number of factors which you need to consider when planning your planting: height, growth habit, time of flowering, flower shape and colour, foliage shape, texture and colour, and secondary attractions such as seed heads.

HEIGHT

It almost goes without saying that you should not put very short plants at the back of the border where you cannot see them. Yet there are exceptions. In a herbaceous border which is planned to be at its best in June, snowdrops, primroses and anemones can be planted all the way through, even at the back, for when they flower there will be almost no growth in front to obscure them. Furthermore, the old idea of growing all the tall plants at the back and all the short ones at the front does give a rather formal, regimented look to the border. By planting some of the taller ones in groups which reach forward in the border you can create a more interesting effect.

HABIT

Plants vary in the way they grow. A border full of plants that develop into rounded hummocks would look strange. On the other

---

The evergreen Gladwyn iris, *Iris foetidissima*, displays spectacular fruits when the seed pods split open (see p. 54)

hand, consciously planting a mixture so that no two plants of the same habit are next to each other will have no spark. Look at the growth habits of the individual plants and treat each case on its own merits.

FLOWERING TIME

Many people like to make gardens which 'look attractive all the year round' and this is perfectly reasonable and possible. But it is exceptionally difficult to achieve this in just one bed or border. For if you plan a relatively small space for year-round interest, at each season there are one or two plants at their peak, yet the border itself never looks stunning – there are always plants which are a long way before or after looking their best. Planning borders to be at their best for a restricted season at least ensures they will be colourful. And even in relatively small gardens, planning several beds or even corners to be at their best at different seasons is a very effective way of organising your planting. This ensures that there is always one area which is at its best while another fades and another is ready to follow on.

FLOWER SHAPE

Flowers come in a huge range of shapes and sizes and are carried in a wide variety of different ways. Daisy shapes, trumpets, spikes – whatever. You can have fun with these in two ways. Contrasting a plant with stiff spikes of flowers such as Salvia × superba with another like Achillea 'Gold Plate', which flowers in flat heads, is very effective (see opposite). Likewise, choosing plants of similar habit but with different individual flowers and in varying colours also works very well and is eye-catching, as, for example, yellow kniphofias and blue veronicas.

FLOWER COLOUR

This is the one aspect of plant association which attracts everyone – and of course it is important. But it is also a trap for the unwary. Many gardeners see the single colour border as a way of taking the angst out of planning. But creating attractive borders around narrow colour themes is much more difficult than it sounds. White is a popular colour theme but only when the border blooms may the realisation dawn that there are many variations of white – and that they do not always go together. One particular irritation can be that unopened buds or fading flowers may take on yellow, blue, green or pink tints. Blue borders are also popular but, again, there are so many different blues! And the purplish ones do not always fit with the sharper shades.

A slightly looser approach can often be successful, one that imposes guidelines but does not restrict you to a single colour. Blue, pink and silver borders work well; so, too, do fiery borders in bronze, red, orange and yellow. Combining a couple of harmonious colours, perhaps with a sympathetic foliage shade, gives the whole border a more relaxed feel, although without abandoning a theme.

FOLIAGE SHAPE AND TEXTURE

A blend of contrasting foliage shape and texture can be very satisfying, especially as foliage lasts for so much longer than flowers. The variety is almost endless. There is the broad, bold foliage of plants like hostas, sword-like irises and lacy ferns. Bergenias are glossy, stachys is woolly, bugles metallic and meconopsis rough.

A splendid contrast in colour and form is achieved through the association of *Salvia × superba* with *Achillea* 'Gold Plate' (see pp. 59 and 41)

Combinations that involve thoughtful use of these qualities repay close inspection.

FOLIAGE COLOUR

Leaves, too, vary in colour. Most, of course, are green but if this gives the impression that they are all the same, this is far from true. The more you look at leaves the more the word 'green' is revealed as encompassing colours that deserve quite different names. In addition to all those greens, leaves come in various yellow tinted shades through to deep gold; in blues through to grey; and in coppers, bronze, purples and reds. Variegated leaves may cover combinations of all these even if the pale-edged or pale-splashed forms are the most common.

This multiplicity of variation can be treated in a number of ways. Some gardeners use it as a theme in itself and plant single-colour, even yellow- or grey-leaved, borders, sometimes realising only too late that these plants also carry flowers. I find the best approach is

Above: hostas are invaluable foliage plants, with leaves in many shades of green. Some, like 'Frances Williams', are beautifully variegated (see p. 52) Opposite: the flower heads of bergenia grow up through the shiny evergreen foliage to bring welcome colour to the garden early in the year

to treat foliage as simply another colour to be worked into the mix. Lasting longer, it provides continuity but needs as careful association with other plants as do flowers.

SECONDARY ATTRACTIONS

Many plants have secondary features which come into their own before or after their prime season, and these can augment or detract from the border on either side of the central display. Autumn colour, fruits and seed heads, tinted early foliage – these are important features which can bring colour to a bed or border out of its main season. The colours and forms at this time of year must either be planned as thoughtfully as for the main season or you must be prepared to take a chance and risk a few surprises. Just to give some hints of possible ways to go about things, here are some examples of effective associations involving hardy perennials. I would urge you, nevertheless, not to follow them slavishly, but to come up with your own ideas and develop your own tastes.

Summer foliage in shade A blue hosta like 'Halcyon', lacy ferns such as *Athyrium filix-femina* with *Iris foetidissima*.

Winter foliage in shade Bold, richly coloured *Bergenia* 'Bressingham Ruby' and the silvery white *Lamium maculatum* 'White Nancy' in front, with the white striped *Iris foetidissima* 'Variegata' behind.

Winter flowers in shade Smaller dark leaved bergenias like 'Abendglut' for background, *Pulmonaria rubra*, winter aconites and snowdrops.

Spring flowers in shade Purple hellebores, white wood anemones and pale blue *Pulmonaria* 'Fruhlingshimmel'.

Spring flowers in sun Limy yellow *Euphorbia characias*, the brighter *Cheiranthus* 'Bredon', apple green *Helleborus argutifolius*, rich purple *Pulsatilla vulgaris* and honesty.

Summer flowers Pink and white *Lavatera* 'Barnsley', blue spikes of *Campanula persicifolia*, *Anaphalis margaritacea* for grey foliage with white flowers to follow, and the long-flowering pink *Geranium endressii* 'Wargrave'.

Blue and yellow flowers Arching shoots of *Mertensia pulmonarioides*, pale lemon *Narcissus* 'Hawera', sparkling blue *Omphalodes cappadocica* 'Cherry Ingram' with yellow-eyed blue violets like

16

Vigorous *Crocosmia* 'Lucifer' opens its fiery red flowers from mid-summer

'Ardross Gem' and perhaps the yellow flowers and red foliage of *Euphorbia amygdaloides* 'Rubra' for contrast.

Fiery flowers *Crocosmia* 'Lucifer' with *Dahlia* 'Bishop of Llandaff' plus orange and rusty heleniums.

Horizontal and vertical Flat heads of *Achillea filipendulina* 'Gold Plate', upright spikes of deep blue *Salvia* 'May Night' with dainty, foamy *Coreopsis* 'Moonbeam' in front.

17

Cultivation

SOILS

There are no soils in which it is impossible to grow perennials; indeed there are plenty of good examples suitable for most soils. The oft-quoted ideal of a rich, well-drained, medium loam is one which few of us can aspire to but we should not be downcast. Moist soils can be improved sufficiently to allow a very wide choice.

Soils which cannot be drained and so remain waterlogged for much of the year may still be planted effectively by choosing the right plants. Dry soils, too, benefit from careful plant choice but are easily improved to suit a wider range.

The enthusaist for perennials is far luckier than the shrub fanatic when it comes to lime. Many of the most sought-after shrubs such as rhododendrons and pieris hate lime and thus are beyond the reach of many gardeners. Perennials are less fussy and although some, like lupins, may prefer an acid soil, failing this they will still thrive.

SITUATION

There is a wide choice of plants available for most situations. This is not so much because hardy perennials are adaptable (though many are) but rather that perennials grow naturally in such diverse habitats and so many kinds are available, that there are always plenty suited to any particular spot. So in sun or shade, wind or sea spray, on slopes or level ground, indeed anywhere you suggest, there are perennials to fit. But since not all are adaptable, it remains important to choose the right plant for the right place. Do not simply put a plant you like into a space you happen to have available.

Furthermore, there are ways of making seemingly inhospitable areas more acceptable to plants. You might build a raised bed to give a greater depth of soil; thin or remove the lower branches of a

A mixed border with the silver foliage of *Stachys lanata* and the giant thistle-like *Onopordon*, combined with frothy lime-green *Alchemilla mollis*

tree to let in more light; or plant evergreens for shelter. Just a little forethought can widen the range of possible plants enormously.

PREPARATION

Thorough preparation of beds and borders is the single most important thing you can do to ensure that your plants thrive. If you wish to grow perennials in mixed borders, then double digging will be valuable – though as much for the shrubs as the perennials. For island beds and herbaceous borders thorough single digging will suffice.

Always consider the drainage. Laying drains is a major job, and if you are surrounded by other gardens where is the run-off to go? A soakaway only has a limited capacity. Sometimes compaction is the cause of poor drainage, and this can be remedied by double digging. Add plenty of organic matter at the same time. I feel that forking it into both the lower spit and the upper spit is preferable to leaving it in layers. In most situations thorough single digging will be quite sufficient.

Organic matter such as well-rotted farmyard manure is excellent, though not always easy to come by. Good garden compost is a close second, and there are various other materials like spent mushroom compost (it must be sterilised), composted bark and the many soil conditioners which have come on the market since we have become aware of the need to avoid using peat on the garden. It will bear restating: do not use peat as a soil conditioner.

The other important job is to remove weeds. They can be removed by hand as you go through. It is imperative to remove all perennial weed roots as any that are left will only cause trouble later – when it is so much more difficult to deal with them.

If the area is obviously weedy, it will pay to deal with the weeds first, before cultivation begins. Spraying with glyphosate will kill most; I find that a second application a fortnight after the first gives the best results. If you prefer, it is just as effective to cover the whole area in opaque black polythene or old carpet to smother weed growth, although this takes much longer to work.

PLANTING

After all the work on the soil, there are final preparations to be done before actually planting. The bed or border should be knocked down roughly level with the fork and then raked to give an even finish. It must then be trodden to ensure there are no air spaces;

otherwise sinkage will be uneven. A little extra levelling may be needed at this stage. A dressing of fertiliser is advisable before planting. Raking in a handful of a general fertiliser such as blood, fish and bone or Growmore to each square yard will give the plants a flying start. If you are planting in the autumn, leave the fertiliser application until the spring as the winter rain will only leach it away before the roots get a chance to use it.

In the days after preparation assemble as many of the plants as you have to hand. Planting can take place whenever the soil is not frozen, sodden or parched. But only in spring or autumn will you be able to plant both pot-grown and bare-root plants together with any to be moved from other parts of the garden. Generally I would suggest September, October, late March or April as the best planting times. My personal instinct is to plant in spring, as growth will start almost at once, whereas in autumn there is no way to protect plants against winter's frost and rain.

Some autumn-flowering plants such as chrysanthemums and Michaelmas daisies are best left until spring unless planted from pots; and even if the rest of the bed is planted in the autumn, it is wise to leave a few others until the winter is over. These include lobelias and penstemons, which are not reliably winter hardy in all areas, and some which object to winter wet like catananche, pyrethrums, anthemis, scabious and gaillardia. Simply mark their sites and leave them in the frame until April.

Choose a day without extremes for planting; cool, still and humid conditions suit both plants and planter. You may have a plan drawn out, but in any event you should have given some thought to the planting scheme before confronting the empty bed at your feet. Set the plants out on the bed where they are to go, preferably marking positions for bare-root plants initially with canes to avoid exposing the roots to the elements. Almost without exception, perennials look better planted in groups of three, five, six, seven or eight than as single plants. This does not necessarily mean buying three of everything, as many newly bought perennials can be knocked out of their containers and immediately split.

Plant small plants with a trowel, large ones with spade. The best general rule is to set them just a fraction lower in the soil than they were previously growing and to firm them well. Plants dug from the open ground, either in the nursery or from your own garden, should have their roots spread out well unless they have a good root ball, in which case this should be retained as far as possible. Work from a board on heavy soil to avoid compaction. Be sure to firm the plants in well, but use fingers in preference to boot, especially on heavy soil. Autumn-set plants will need checking during the winter as frost and heavy rain can leave them loose in the soil or expose the roots. Ensure the plants are well labelled.

After planting, water each plant thoroughly. It is also a good idea to add a liquid feed to help give them a flying start. The simplest way to water a large planting is with a sprinkler, but try to avoid wasting water. I usually start by watering in from a can. It is vital to prevent container-grown plants from drying out in the summer after planting.

When planting and watering are completed the soil should be lightly pricked over to leave it looking neat. Finally, if weed-free organic matter is available in liberal quantities, the whole bed can be mulched.

The story is similar when planting a group of perennials or adding a single plant to an existing planting. The site should be forked over and organic matter mixed in, followed, as before, by treading and application of fertiliser. Beware of hidden bulbs and self-sown seedlings which may be disturbed.

MULCHING

Regular mulching makes an invaluable contribution to the success of hardy perennial plantings. A good mulch helps retain moisture, thus removing the need for quite so much irrigation, keeps down weeds, feeds the plants and in the long run improves the soil.

Mulch should be well rotted, friable and weed free. Only the best garden compost meets all three criteria – the third being the most often wanting. Farmyard or stable manure is probably the best choice but it may need stacking to allow it to finish rotting. Spent mushroom compost is excellent, though limy, but it must be sterilised to to kill mushroom fly larvae. Peat is now not an option as a mulch but the many soil-conditioning peat substitutes are ideal. Never use lawn mowings as they invariably contain weed seeds, especially annual meadow grass.

The time to mulch depends to some extent on the type of planting. In a herbaceous border or island bed, early spring is ideal, but in mixed and cottage plantings, where there may be very early plants like snowdrops and aconites, autumn is preferable.

FEEDING

If you prepare well and are able to use a rich mulch on a regular basis, feeding may be totally unnecessary. If you use no mulch at all, feeding is essential. For many gardeners, supply and demand governs the frequency of mulching any given bed, so mulching one year and feeding the next is a reasonable compromise. A handful of blood, fish and bone or Growmore to the square yard in early spring, raked in lightly, is all the plants need. These are general fertilisers that many gardeners possess and which can be bought economically in large sacks. I find that various specific feeds are unnecessary, although sometimes individual plants benefit from an occasional liquid feed.

WATERING

In recent years a succession of drier summers have led to widespread restrictions on the use of sprinklers. The best way to reduce the need for watering is to add plenty of organic matter during preparation, to mulch well and regularly, and to choose plants carefully for the different situations in your garden.

When it comes to using the sprinkler (standing with hosepipe in hand, or tying it to the handle of a fork are equally useless methods) a thorough watering every couple of weeks is far more effective than a skimpy one every couple of days. Choose a sprinkler to suit your beds. Long, straight formal borders are best watered with a square pattern, oscillating sprinkler, while for beds in sweeping curves a pulse sprinkler which waters circles and segments of circles is less wasteful. Do not forget that you need a licence from your local water company for a sprinkler.

WEEDING

Weeds need particular attention in the preparation and early years of herbaceous plantings, but once established, even the most upright of hardy perennials should produce a sufficiently dense cover to smother the majority. Assuming the roots of perennial weeds are removed during preparation, mulching will deal with most weeds as long as the mulch itself is weed free. In the absence of mulching, hoeing is effective early in the season, even in mature borders, although self-sown seedlings are likely to be decapitated along with the weeds. There are two rules to all weeding which apply here as anywhere else: never let any weeds set seed and always remove perennial weeds the moment you spot them.

Occasionally bindweed, ground elder or other particularly tenacious weeds appear in the clumps of perennials and can quickly take a hold. The simplest trick is to paint the leaves with a

23

weedkiller aproved for use in this way. Bindweed can be untwisted first. However, if perennial weeds appear under a newly set plant, it is better to dig up the plant, remove the weed roots and then put the plant back.

STAKING

In island beds, the majority of the plants grown are usually short, stocky and self supporting. But tall and weak-stemmed plants, those in open positions and in traditional borders often need support and this must be done as unobtrusively as possible. Brushwood (pea sticks) is the traditional supporting material. Hazel is by far the best as it comes in convenient flat, fan-shaped sprays. Birch is sometimes more readily available but you need bigger quantities and it is more obtrusive. Neither is easy to come by, although local nature conservation groups who may be managing woodlands are often a good source.

Surround the plants with the brushwood and loop string around the outside and across the middle to secure it well. The top 12 in (30 cm) can be broken over to a horizontal position for the shoots to grow through. Alternatively, set bamboo canes 12–18 in (30–45 cm) apart around the edge of a group, wind string round them and cross it over between the canes. For tall single-stemmed plants like delphiniums, single canes are sometimes used, each stem being tied in individually with two or three loose ties of soft string. Wire supports in a number of styles are now available and are convenient, unobtrusive and very effective. They can be expensive to buy but should last for many years. Whichever system you choose, the supports must be the right height and must be in place early in the season. Judging the height can be tricky as growth can vary from year to year. Most plants need support to about half or two-thirds of their eventual height, or to just below their leafy growth. In gardens with large borders, it is useful to record the correct staking heights in a notebook for future reference.

Stakes should always be in position early in the season so that plants are supported as they grow rather than propped up after collapsing. This can mean that for a few weeks canes or brushwood are more obtrusive than you would like, but the shoots weave through them as they grow and they will be well hidden later.

The soft ferny foliage of delphiniums soon covers the stakes necessary to keep these tall plants upright

REPLANTING

Many perennials need regular lifting and replanting to keep them in good health and flowering well. They can be lifted in autumn or spring, choosing the strongest and healthiest pieces from the outside of the clump for replanting (see Propagation, page 31). Various plants need this treatment for different reasons. Shasta daisies (*Leucanthemum x superbum*), heucheras and bergenias tend to grow out of the ground, exposing woody growth. Michaelmas daisies (*Aster*) produce the best flowers from strong young shoots. Monardas, crocosmias, some campanulas, achilleas, some asters and others simply creep too far and need restraining.

Conversely, there are some plants that are best left undisturbed to make impressive clumps. These include hostas, hellebores, rheums and peonies.

DEADHEADING

The flowering period of many plants can be extended by regular removal of dead flowering shoots just above the first set of leaves below them. Salvias, phlox and anthemis will usually bloom for longer, while delphiniums and Shasta daisies will look much neater. Some plants will flower again later in the year if the flowering stems are cut out entirely. Many more will grow fresh, attractive new foliage if cut down right to the ground when flowering is over. Plants which benefit in this way include astrantias, achilleas, doronicums, Oriental poppies (*Papaver*) and many cranesbills (*Geranium*). Apart from improving their appearance, all plants benefit from deadheading as it diverts their energy from seed production to fattening up the roots. It also prevents prolific seeders such as achilleas from producing vast numbers of unwanted seedlings.

There is one situation, of course, where dead heads should not be removed. If the seed heads themselves are attractive they are best left on the plant right through until spring. Grasses, sedums and astilbes fall into this category.

END OF SEASON

At some point in the dormant season borders need tidying: some people like to do it in the autumn, others in the spring. Autumn is the traditional time. When the last Michaelmas daisies and other asters are over, you can usually get to work – unless there are naturalised colchicums or autumn flowering crocus in the border! First remove the stakes and supports, then cut out dead stems at ground level and get rid of all the debris; the woodiest material is ideal for the base of the compost heap. Next, remove weeds and gather up fallen leaves, which can also go on the compost heap. Any replanting or dividing can now be done and labels checked and re-written. Fork the whole border over lightly to neaten it up and expose soil pests to your friendly robin. Finally, apply a mulch.

There are two problems with this autumn treatment. Late autumn-flowering plants are becoming increasingly popular and thus may still be in flower in November. Also, dead stems can look very attractive in winter, especially when coated with frost. So you may prefer to leave the whole job until the spring.

Geranium renardii is one of the more unusual cranesbills, ideal for the front of a sunny border (see p.49)

CULTIVATION CALENDAR

Spring
○ Do not tread on heavy soil after rain.
○ Apply a general fertiliser such as blood, fish and bone or Growmore.
○ Plant newly received plants; heel them in for planting later if conditions are bad.
○ Stake any plants that need support; see to early flowering subjects like peonies first.
○ Tie delphiniums and other spire plants to canes as they grow.
○ Lift and divide plants that resent the process in autumn or which were overlooked.
○ Hoe between clumps if the border was not mulched in autumn.
○ Check that perennial weeds are not emerging in the centre of clumps.
○ Beware of emerging bulbs when working amongst the plants.
○ Deadhead early-flowering plants like doronicums as necessary.
○ Water newly planted borders or groups if necessary.
○ Fill gaps with appropriate summer bedding plants and hardy or half-hardy annuals.
○ Prevent slug damage to hostas and other susceptible plants using pellets or other treatments.
○ Look out for aphids, capsids, thrips, caterpillars and other pests and treat accordingly.
○ Order new plants for autumn and spring planting.

Summer
○ Check that plants are not evading their supports.
○ Lift and divide flag irises after flowering.
○ Deadhead as flowers fade; pay special attention to columbines (Aquilegia), achilleas and other prolific seeders.
○ Cut back Oriental poppies (Papaver), astrantias and similar plants to encourage a flush of fresh foliage.
○ Water newly planted borders or single groups if necessary. Be prepared to spot-water flagging plants.
○ Watch for weeds which have evaded the hoe, mulch or steely eye.
○ Continue to look out for pests, mildew and grey mould.
○ Order new plants for autumn and spring planting.

Autumn
○ Continue to deadhead to prevent carpets of self-sown seedlings.
○ Plant new borders and groups, lift and divide most perennials.
○ Start digging and preparing new beds as soon as possible.

Winter
○ Cut down dead stems and clear away to the compost heap. Do it early or late as you choose.
○ Keep off the border when the soil is wet.
○ Order new plants for spring planting.

Mixed asters include *Aster × frikartii* and Michaelmas daisies (see p. 42), seen here with a yellow kniphofia

Propagation

One of the great attractions of hardy herbaceous perennials is that most are so easy to propagate. Many can be raised from seed with little or no special conditions or equipment. Most can simply be lifted, divided and replanted, whereupon they will grow away well. Some propagate themselves all too easily.

DIVISION

Almost all hardy perennials can be divided, although some resent it and some increase so slowly that division is only possible after several years and yields few young plants. The process is easiest with plants like Michaelmas daisies (*Aster*) with their loose, fibrous roots system, while peonies and hellebores are more difficult. In almost all cases, unless you need to produce as many new plants as possible there will be some old, tired and woody growth which is best discarded. The youngest growth, usually at the edge of the clump, is the best for propagation.

Most plants can be lifted and divided in the autumn. First dig up the clump using a border fork, or digging fork if necessary. Shake off a little of the soil so that you can see what you are doing and then decide how to approach it. A few plants such as flag irises can simply be pulled and broken to yield pieces suitable for replanting. Plants with open, fibrous growth can be split using the famous two forks method. (It helps if the two forks are the same size, so you may need to borrow one.) The same method can be adopted for smaller plants such as violas by using handforks.

If you find it difficult to see exactly where to divide tightly congested clumps of plants like hellebores or polyanthus, wash the soil off, using a hosepipe, and cut the plant into individual crowns with a knife or secateurs.

Plants with exceptionally tough, dense growth such as hostas can be treated differently (see below). When you have your small divisions ready, either plant them directly into the border in

---

Foxgloves (*Digitalis*) are best raised from seed, while clumps of hosta can be divided *in situ* with a knife to avoid disturbing the roots more than necessary

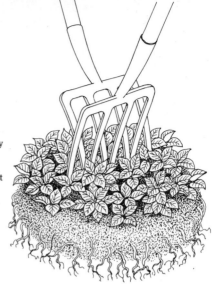

The two forks method. Push the two forks vertically through the middle of the clump, back to back; then break the clump in two by working the handles together and pulling them apart. The process can be repeated to break up the clump further, at which point it is usually possible to pull off strong shoots for replanting.

improved soil or line them out for a season to make bigger plants before moving them to their flowering positions.

Finally, do not be afraid to divide plants as soon as they are received from the nursery. Many plants in 4–5 in (10–13 cm) pots, and sometimes those in smaller ones, will yield a couple of splits or can even be divided into three or four pieces straight away. This applies especially to plants like achilleas, schizostylis and crocosmias which produce short runners.

Using a spade. Alternatively, use a spade to cut vertically through the middle of the clump. This can even be done with the plant still in the ground so that one half at least is disturbed relatively little. It sounds brutal but large clumps possess enough crowns to be able to spare one or two being sliced off.

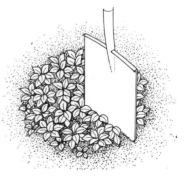

Using a knife. If you do not wish to disturb a specimen clump, use an old bread knife to cut and remove a triangular segment like a slice from a cake. Then fill the resulting hole with fresh soil.

Propagating from thongy roots

1. Lift the plant, wash off some of the soil and cut off a few roots roughly the thickness of a pencil and about 2–3 in (5–7.5 cm) long. Cut the top square and the bottom slanted so that you can tell the top from the bottom.

2. Fill a 5 in (13 cm) pot with the same compost as used for cuttings, leaving a 1 in (2.5 cm) gap at the top. Insert the cuttings vertically in dibber holes so that the top of each cutting is level with the surface of the compost.

3. Top with ½ in (12 mm) of grit and water in well. Then leave the pot in a cold frame for the roots to develop shoots. In spring they can be potted up individually and planted out when large enough.

CUTTINGS

Many hardy perennials can be easily increased from stem cuttings although they must be taken at the right time. Spring is the season for most species. As a rule, the shoots should be 3–4 in (7.5–10 cm) long, and not hollow. In practice this means severing them close to the crown, even with a heel, using a very sharp pair of secateurs or a sharp knife. It is difficult to be precise as to exact timing, for this will vary with the plant and the season, so it pays to watch the plants you wish to increase from February onwards. Those with flowers and leaves which all spring from the base, like hellebores and hostas, are not suitable. This method can only work with plants which have recognisable stems, such as delphiniums and anthemis.

Collect the cuttings in a polythene bag, labelling them as you go. Ensure they are trimmed cleanly and remove the lower leaves and any damaged ones. They can be inserted in a compost made up of 50 per cent proprietary cuttings compost and 50 per cent perlite or grit. I find most composts stay too wet unless grit is added. Use 3 in (7.5 cm) pots, 5 in (13 cm) half-pots or half-trays depending on the size and number of the cuttings you have. Bury them deep enough to hold them upright, but no deeper, and place them in an unheated propagator in the greenhouse or on the windowsill. Ensure they are not subject to strong sun or they may scorch; look out for botrytis (grey mould). When rooted, pot them up individually, harden them off if necessary and grow them on outside or in a frame until ready for planting.

ROOT CUTTINGS

Certain plants are not easy to divide or root from stem cuttings, while for others these methods are, for various reasons, unsuitable. Some of these plants, however, root readily from winter root

Propagating from fibrous roots

1. If you only want a few plants, there is no need to lift the whole plant, simply scrape away the soil from the roots and cut off sections of fibrous root 3–4 in (7.5–10 cm) long.

2. Lay these out flat on the surface of compost in seed trays and cover with about ¼ in (6 mm) of compost.

3. If you require more plants, lift the whole plant and prepare as many roots as you need. Then gather them into bundles of about then, tie with raffia or soft twine, and insert vertically as if they were one fat root cutting. When they begin to shoot, separate them for potting individually.

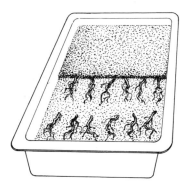

cuttings. They can be divided into two groups, the fat and the fibrous.

Those with fat thongy roots include such plants as Oriental poppies (*Papaver*), anchusa, globe thistles (*Echinops*) and *Crambe cordifolia*.

Plants with fine, fibrous roots such as phlox require a slightly different method (see above).

SEED

Many of the plants mentioned later in this book can be raised from seed and for some this is the ideal method. However, many

34

cultivars will not produce identical seedlings, and must therefore be increased by division or cuttings.

Plants which I particularly recommend that you raise from seed are: alchemillas, alliums, columbines (*Aquilega*), delphiniums, fox-gloves (*Digitalis*), hellebores, peas (*Lathyrus*), lupins, meconopsis and pulsatilla. Even some of these, however, are best divided if you have special cultivars.

Most perennials can be sown in spring and are not all that fussy. John Innes Seed Compost, if you can be sure of good quality, or a soil-less seed compost will suit them. Use a small pot, 5 in (13 cm) half-pot or half-size seed tray according to the number of plants you wish to raise. Sow them in March or April in just the same way as you would bedding plants and then place the pots in a propagator, warm or frost-free greenhouse, cold greenhouse, cold frame or even outside in a sheltered spot. The warmer the spot, the quicker they will come up. If you raise a lot of half-hardy annuals from seed, you may be short of space early in the season. In that case sowing can be left until May or June and you should still get good-sized plants by the end of the season. After germination, prick out into trays or individual pots. As the seedlings mature, you can either plant them straight into beds and borders or line them out first to grow on for a while. Early sowing and lining out is especially val-uable with plants like lupins and delphiniums, seed of which is often sold in mixtures. These will usually produce a small flower spike late in their first summer and this will enable you to check the colours.

It is often recommended that seed of perennials be sown in summer in the open ground. This works well if you have plenty of seed, and packets of foxgloves, for example, are often generously filled. But the garden environment is a dangerous one for seeds, and as so many packets contain just a few seeds it pays to give them the protection of a pot and some special compost rather than let them take their chance in the outside world.

Although this method works well for many seeds, some either need to be sown fresh or need a period of cold before they will germinate. Sowing hellebores in July can give you almost 100 per cent germination, usually before Christmas; if you keep the seed until January or buy it then from a seed company, very few are likely to germinate. A number of other plants such as pulsatillas and many primulas and gentians are also best sown fresh, but then must be left in a cold frame or north-facing spot outside where they will get the frost in winter. This is needed to encourage germination which will usually occur in the spring.

Pests and Diseases

Compared with indoor plants, hardy perennials are not troubled by many pests and diseases, although some of those which are troublesome can be especially debilitating. If your plants are grown well, they are generally less likely to be attacked, and less likely to be killed if they are. Growing plants in a soil and situation which suits them, giving them the individual care they need, feeding, watering and mulching will give them strength to ride out any attack which may occur. Fortunately, hardy perennials are tough plants, so perhaps we should show a little tolerance. There is no need to rush for the sprayer at the first sign of an aphid or to fill it with the most lethal potion on the garden centre shelf. Pinching off diseased shoots, physically squashing caterpillars and similar basic methods can be very successful if attended to regularly.

PESTS

Aphids
The most common pest, aphids come in a wide range of sizes and colours and debilitate plants by sucking sap; they also transmit virus diseases. The fat grey ones which attack lupins are especially prolific.
Organic control: Squash with fingers, or use soap-based insecticides.
Chemical control: Spray with pirimicarb which spares most beneficial insects.

Capsids
Insects up to ¼ in (6 mm) long suck sap from the shoot tips and the leaves develop small irregular holes as they expand. Most common in late spring and summer.
Organic control: Pinch out shoot tips, clear away debris and garden waste.
Chemical control: Spray with malathion, pirimiphos-methyl or dimethoate, concentrating on shoot tips.

Euphorbia characias subsp. *wulfenii* 'Lambrook Gold' is one of the most stately and impressive herbaceous perennials (see p. 48)

Earwigs

The familiar earwigs chew petals, especially of double and fleshy flowers like chrysanthemums, dahlias, delphiniums and Michael-mas daisies; they also sometimes eat flower buds and young leaves. *Organic control*: Clear rubbish, trap insects under old sacking or cardboard, up-end flower pots stuffed with straw on canes as traps. *Chemical control*: Spray at dusk with malathion or pirimiphos-methyl when damage is seen.

Leather jackets

These daddy-long-legs larvae are especially common when new beds are made in lawns. Grey-brown larvae up to 2 in (5 cm) long feed on roots and young shoots, especially in spring.
Organic control: Fork over new beds a couple of times to allow birds to get at the larvae.
Chemical control: Generally impractical although soil insecticides such as bromophos, phoxin or gamma HCH can be forked into the soil around especially valuable plants and slug pellets containing methiocarb may have some effect.

Slugs and snails

Probably the most destructive of all pests, especially in damp springs, they eat young shoots of a wide variety of plants as well as tubers and bulbs.
Organic control: Clear away debris which provides daytime hiding places. Use slug killers based on aluminium sulphate. Hand pick by torchlight on mild damp evenings.
Chemical control: Use slug pellets containing methiocarb or metaldehyde. Do not leave in large heaps; single pellets at 4in (10 cm) intervals are just as effective.

Wireworms

Orange-brown larvae about 1 in (2.5 cm) long tunnel into stems, roots, bulbs and tubers, particularly in spring. Most common on newly cultivated ground.
Organic control: Cultivate ground well before planting to allow birds to feed. Keep weeds under control.
Chemical control: Work soil insecticides such as bromophos, phoxin or gamma HCH into the soil around special plants.

DISEASES

Stem and leaf rots

A variety of different rots attack stems, leaves and flowers of many different plants including chrysanthemums, delphiniums, carn-

38

ations (*Dianthus*) and peonies. The result is rotting crowns, grey mould on foliage and flowers, brown rots on stems and leaves.
Organic control: Difficult, but improving drainage can sometimes help. Spray with colloidal sulphur.
Chemical control: Spray with benomyl, carbendazium or thiophanate-methyl and repeat according to the manufacturer's instructions. Dust crowns with dry Bordeaux powder.

Leaf spots
A number of plants including peonies, hellebores, aquilegias, campanulas and irises can suffer from various leaf-spotting problems, especially in wet conditions.
Organic control: Difficult: colloidal sulphur will deal with some.
Chemical control: Diseases on different plants respond to different fungicides, Bordeaux mixture, benomyl and mancozeb are among the most effective.

Powdery Mildew
A white powdery coating spreads over stems and foliage, leaves eventually go yellow and drop off. In dry conditions and in crowded borders this disease can attack a wide variety of plants. Although the appearance is generally similar, each plant often has its own specific mildew which will not spread to different plants.
Organic control: Spray with colloidal sulphur.
Chemical control: Spray with benomyl, bupirimate with triforine, carbendazium, fenarinol, propiconazole or thiophanate-methyl.

Root and foot rots
Many apparently unexplained deaths of a wide range of plants are the result of these rots which are caused by a variety of fungi. Wilting or feeble growth may be the first sign of trouble.
Organic control: Thriving plants are much less susceptible, so growing plants well is half the battle. Dig up and burn infected plants and replace with a plant of a different type. Improve cultivation, especially soil quality, drainage and pH levels.
Chemical control: There are no direct chemical controls.

Virus
Virus diseases are becoming increasingly common especially on hostas, lilies, primroses, wallflowers (*Cheiranthus*), chrysanthemums and delphiniums. Symptoms vary but include poor growth, distorted foliage, pale streaking or mottled leaves, poor flowering, difficulty in propagation and streaky and distorted flowers.
Organic control: Dig up and burn affected plants. Control the aphids which often spread the viruses.
Chemical control: None.

Choosing from the vast range of hardy perennials available to gardeners is a thankless task. There will always be individual favourites which are not included or given but scant attention. When in doubt, however, I have given preference to those whose popularity is increasing. This is, after all, intended as an introductory book; there are comprehensive volumes for gardeners who crave information on more plants and in more detail.

Acanthus Sumptuous foliage plants with large, glossy leaves making impressive but often invasive clumps 4–5 ft (1.2–1.5 m) high. A. mollis 'Latifolius' has floppy, broadly divided leaves. In A. spinosus the leaves are broader, deeper green and tipped with spines, while the slightly silvered 'Spinosissimus' is more finely cut and even more spiny. All are happy in sun or shade but flower best in the sun, their spikes of pink or purple two-lipped flowers rising through the foliage in late summer.

Achillea Easy but often invasive plants, good for unimproved soils. All have flat heads of flowers over attractive, finely cut foliage and thrive in most soils in at least half a day's sun. A. millefolium and its various hybrids, 2–3 ft (60–90 cm), can be invasive but are excellent in new gardens. Many fade horribly but exceptions include 'Forncett Fletton' (opposite) in orangey brick red, 'Hoffnung' in sandy yellow and the dark purplish red 'Burgundy'. 'Moonshine' is a more clumpy hybrid with grey foliage and pale yellow flowers. A. filipendulina 'Gold Plate' (see p. 13), is taller and more stately at 4 ft (1.2 m) with broad, bright yellow heads which look wonderful behind upright salvias. The white buttons of A. ptarmica 'The Pearl', 2–3 ft (60–90 cm), are pretty but the plant runs and seeds rather too freely.

Aconitum Summer- and autumn-flowering plants with good foliage and spikes of hooded flowers, usually in blue. 'Bressingham Spire', 3 ft (90 cm), is purplish blue, 'Blue Sceptre', 2 ft (60 cm), has blue and white bicolored flowers; both are self supporting. 'Newry Blue', 5ft (1.5 m), is much more stately but needs support. Rather different are the creamy flowered 'Ivorine' and the yellowish A. vulparia which will scramble through shrubs or fall through an earlier

The warm orangey tones of Achillea 'Forncett Fletton' associate well with mauve flowers, such as heliotrope or Michaelmas daisies

flowering perennial. Good soil and full sun or partial shade suits them well. The tuberous roots are poisonous.

Alchemilla Almost every garden now features the limy yellow flowers and slightly downy leaves of the delightful A. *mollis* – but it does self-sow freely. Wonderful in front of blue irises or with diascias, but you should be ruthless with the seedlings or they will crowd out other plants. Thrives in most reasonable soils and situations.

Anemone The Japanese anemones are invaluable late-flowering plants and though difficult to move and often slow to establish, once settled they spread well, sometimes too well. All those listed under A. *hupehensis*, A. *japonica* and A. × *hybrida* are very similar with their running roots, deeply toothed foliage and elegant stems carrying single or semi-double flowers in various pinks or white. The plant usually listed simply as A. × *hybrida*, 5 ft (1.5 m), is shimmering pink. 'Honorine Jobert' is similar but purest white. 'Bressingham Glow' is half as tall and a semi-double warm pink. All appreciate full sun, a heavy soil and space to run.

Anthemis Easy and reliable daisies in two groups, both growing well in sun and any reasonably well-drained soil. The various forms of A. *tinctoria*, 3 ft (90 cm), flower exuberantly for many weeks in summer. 'Grallach Gold' is rich yellow, 'E. C. Buxton' paler and sharper; both need staking with brushwood. They are often short-lived, but cutting back hard when the flowers fade is a help, as is regular replanting with the strongest divisions. Lower and more spreading is the invaluable A. *cupaniana*, 12 in (30 cm), with fine, silvery foliage and white daisies from spring to autumn.

Aquilegia Columbines come in a great variety, the only constant factor being their promiscuous tendency to hybridise. New seed or plants from a reliable source are the only ways to ensure correctly named stock. There are many hybrid selections from the compact Music, 15 in (38 cm), to the McKana Hybrids, 3 ft (90 cm), while the fully double pink, white and green 'Nora Barlow' is an old favourite. All these thrive in any rich but well-drained soil in sun or partial shade but they are not long-lived. For species like the red and yellow A. *canadensis*, 2–3 ft (60–80 cm), and the deep olive green A. *viridiflora*, 15 in (38 cm), good drainage is even more necessary.

Aster The Michaelmas daisies are a mixed lot – some fine plants but others tall and floppy; many suffer from mildew. Some of the New England asters, A. *novae-angliae*, 4 ft (1.2 m), are disease and pest resistant and more or less self-supporting; try the warm-toned 'Harrington's Pink', the positively lurid pink 'Andenken an Alma Potschke' and the pure white 'Herbstschnee' ('Autumn Snow') (see p. 44). The true Michaelmas daisy, A. *novi-belgii*, is more variable

42

and includes dwarfs like the 10 in (25 cm) 'Lady in Blue', but some are prone to mildew. These make up only one group; among the many other invaluable asters are the lavender-blue *A.* × *frikartii* 'Mönch', 18 in (45 cm) (see p. 29), which flowers all summer and autumn, and *A. lateriflorus* 'Horizontalis', 2 ft (60 cm), with clouds of tiny lilac and pink flowers. All are tolerant plants thriving in any reasonable soil and a sunny situation; they are best divided every three or four years.

Astilbe Tough, densely spreading plants with good foliage and self-supporting spires of foamy flowers. They come in reds, pinks and white and range in height from 12 in (30 cm) to 4 ft (1.2 m). Astilbes revel in wet or water-retentive soil and full sun but will also do well in slightly drier spots if given a little shade. 'Sprite', 12 in (30 cm), is pearly pink with metallic foliage, 'Fanal', 18 cm (45 cm), is deep red while 'Deutschland', 2 ft (60 cm), is white and 'Amethyst', 3 ft (90 cm), is lilac-pink.

Astrantia Easy to grow, self-supporting, and self-seeding plants with intriguing pincushion flowers surrounded by a ruff of bracts. They are also blessed with good weed-suppressing foliage and are happy in any reasonable soil in sun or dappled shade. The naming is a little confused but among those to look out for are *A. major* with greenish white flowers and *A. maxima* with a pink-tinted cushion and pink bracts. 'Shaggy', also known as 'Margery Fish', has especially well-developed bracts. 'Hadspen Blood' is deep red. 'Sunningdale Variegated' (see p. 44) has yellow- and cream-margined foliage. All reach about 2 ft (60 cm).

Bergenia Sometimes known as elephant's ears, from the broad, rounded foliage, these tough evergreen perennials are splendid for early colour though the flowers are sometimes frosted. Their foliage is valuable all the year round. For good foliage choose 'Bressingham Ruby', the crimson-flowered 'Abendglut' and *B. cordifolia* 'Purpurea' with their rich winter colour. Others to look for are the dwarf pink 'Baby Doll', the big and bold crimson-flowered 'Ballawley' and the stunning pure white 'Beethoven'. Bergenias are sometimes relegated to the driest of shade where they survive but do not thrive. Good soil and sun produces the best leaves and impressive early spring flowering.

Campanula A huge group covering tall plants for the back of the border to neat edgers. They come mainly in blue or white, although there a few pinks and reds. *Campanula lactiflora* 5–6 ft (1.5–1.8 m), is one of the tallest with straight stems breaking into bushy heads of flowers. 'Prichard's Variety' is purplish blue and there is also a white form. The lovely blue *C. persicifolia*, 3 ft (90 cm), is more

43

manageable, its slender stems lined with elegant open bells. There is a white form as well as doubles, semi-doubles and cup-and-saucer types in both blue and white. The cup-and-saucer 'Hampstead White' is charming. Coming down in scale again is a group with a creeping habit and tubular flowers, speckled inside. *C. punctata*, 12–18 in (30–45cm), has pink-tinted flowers with darker spots inside, *C. takesimana*, 2 ft (60 cm), is lilac-tinted with maroon spots. For the very front, *C. carpatica*, 9–12 in (23–30 cm), has cup-shaped flowers over mounds of neat foliage. There are many cultivars, from the deep blue 'Karl Foerster' to 'White Clips'. Most like sun or partial shade and any reasonable soil that is not too waterlogged – in fact the conditions to be found in most gardens. They can be prone to slug damage and it pays to deadhead promptly to encourage a second flush.

Chrysanthemum Now mostly correctly called *Dendranthema*, the garden chrysanthemums are among the most valuable of late-flowering plants. Those in the Rubellum group, 2 ft (60 cm), are especially free-flowering and reliable and include 'Clara Curtis' in a clear pink and 'Duchess of Edinburgh' in coppery red. The hardy hybrids vary from the 4 ft (1.2 m) 'Emperor of China' with silvery pink flowers in November to the 2 ft (60 cm) 'Mei-Kyo' with neat dark pink buttons. There are plenty more, almost all good. Two other fine species, both with single white daisies, are the neat, very late-flowered, 12 in (30 cm) *C. yezoense* (now *Dendranthema yezoense*) and at the other extreme the 6 ft (1.8 m) *C. uliginosum* (now *Leucanthemella serotina*). Earlier than all these are the Shasta daisies (now *Leucanthemum × superbum*), with large, white, anemone-centred or double flowers. They are stiff and upright and need something bushy in front to cover their stems. 'Starburst' is a large single, 'Snowcap' is only 12 in (30 cm) tall, 'Phyllis Smith' has rather a frilly look with narrow petals, 'Cobham Gold' is creamy centred, 'Esther Read' is short and fully double. Most reach about 3 ft (90 cm). All are at their best in full sun or when shaded from the east and in a good soil. Few will need staking unless grown in too shady a spot.

Above left: New England asters, such as *Aster novae-angliae* 'Herbstschnee', are reliable and welcome for their late-flowering habit (see p.42)
Above right: feathery astilbes multiply quickly, and even the taller cultivars do not require staking. They flower throughout the summer
Below left: a clump of *Astrantia* 'Sunningdale Variegated' brings brightness to a garden border with its attractive foliage
Below right: the herbaceous clematis *C. integrifolia* has silvery seedheads which continue the period of interest after the petals fall

Clematis The best known of these unsung heroes are *C. heraclei-folia*, 3 ft (90 cm), and *C. integrifolia*, 2 ft (60 cm) (see p. 44), but there are many other good but almost unknown species. The former makes a spreading plant with clusters of blue flowers in the upper leaf joints: 'Wyevale' is the one to look for. *C. integrifolia* is rather floppier, needs a shrub for support, and has the apparently un-promising trait of carrying just one flower at the tip of each shoot. Fortunately, some of the cultivars like 'Olgae' have branched flower heads. These are good border plants for sun and any reasonable soil, tolerant and strong, but generally in need of thoughtful support.

Crocosmia Vigorous spreaders, most of which are better than the montbretia so often seen in cottage gardens. 'Lucifer', 4 ft (1.2 m) (see p. 14), has arching shoots lined with tubular fiery red flowers and boasts pleated sword-shaped foliage; 'Star of the East', 3 ft (90 cm), has outward-facing apricot yellow flowers on upright shoots; 'Solfaterre', 18 in (45 cm), has smoky bronze foliage and yellow flowers. There are many more. Although most are tough and tend to spread well, all prefer a soil that is not too limy and are at their best in a slightly moist climate. Some are tender in colder areas.

Delphinium These are among the most popular and impressive of the taller border perennials, but are often seen in poor forms raised from second-rate seed stocks. Grow cultivars obtained from specialists or the best seed selections. The best seed-raised selections are the New Century Hybrids, Blackmore & Langdon Strain and Southern Noblemen, 5 ft (1.5 m), all originating in Britain; the American Pacific Giants are less hardy and rather vari-able. Even with these selections it pays to grow the young plants in rows for a year and then pick the best, in preferred colours, for moving to the border. The plants raised from single colour seed selections will vary slightly in shade. All need full sun, a good fertile soil, protection against slugs in the spring and secure staking to avoid calamities. Cut them down after flowering and be prepared to spray against mildew.

Dianthus Garden pinks, 12 in (30 cm), come in such a profusion of cultivars that recommending the best is far from easy. They can conveniently be divided into the old-fashioned pinks, which are mostly scented but once-flowering, and the modern pinks, which tend to flower for longer but may have less scent. Most are double flowered and all have the added benefit of grey-blue foliage in varying degrees. Of the older ones I like the wonderfully scented 'Mrs Sinkins' in pure white, though the flowers are untidy; 'Sops in

Wine' in white with an almost black edging; and 'Brympton Red' in crimson marbled with an even deeper shade. Of the modern ones the dark-eyed, pale pink 'Doris' is well known and there are a number of other good cultivars with forenames. 'Devon Cream' is an unusual creamy shade with a hint of pink, and 'Huntsman' is deep red. All thrive in sunny, well-drained places and love lime. They are ideal edgers.

Diascia These long-flowering sprawlers, 10–12 in (25–30 cm), are good in most soils in sunny places but the colour range is limited to various pink shades. Although vigorous, they die out if not divided and the best pieces replanted almost every year. They are not hardy in the coldest areas. 'Ruby Field' is more a deep pink than ruby, D. vigilis is a lovely pale pink while D. integerrima is probably the darkest.

Dicentra A mixed genus, including creeping woodlanders, early border plants and even climbers. Bleeding heart, D. spectabilis, 2 ft (60 cm), is a wonderful plant with pink or white flowers swinging from arching stems. The young growth is both early and rather soft so is easily damaged by frost; a west-facing border is ideal. Many of the woodland types have greyish foliage and are great colonisers. 'Stuart Boothman' has soft pink lockets hanging over grey, much divided foliage. In 'Snowflakes', the foliage is greener and less divided and the flowers are white; 'Bacchanal' is deep red. All make classy ground cover in partial or full shade if the soil is not dry.

Doronicum Among the most brilliant of early flowers with cheerful bright yellow daisies in April and May. D. caucasicum 'Magnificum' is a good seed-raised form, 'Miss Mason' is a reliable old cultivar with good foliage; both reach about 2 ft (60 cm). 'Spring Beauty' is a little shorter and double flowered. All thrive in sun or partial shade and any good soil. They are best moved in autumn.

Echinops Tall spiny plants with silvery stems and globular heads of blue flowers. Wonderful at the back of the border but they may need support. Best in full sun, they thrive in poor soil and are inclined to run. E. ritro, 4 ft (1.2 m), is steely blue, even in bud, with silver-backed green leaves. E. bannaticus 'Taplow Blue' is slightly taller and is altogether greyer in foliage and stem with richer blue flowers.

Epimedium Increasingly popular creeping woodlanders, 10–15 in (25–38 cm), with open sprays of intriguing spidery flowers and attractively tinted spring foliage. Many new kinds are now appearing. Most are deciduous but a few have evergreen foliage and these include E. perralderianum with glossy leaves and bright yellow flowers. Almost all the deciduous sorts are worth growing, but I would pick these: *E. grandiflorum* has a number of cultivars and both 'Rose Queen' and 'White Queen' are delightful; *E. davidii* has long-spurred, bright yellow flowers; and *E. × rubrum* (below) has especially well-tinted young foliage and deep pink flowers to match. All prefer a cool, dappled spot with leafy or peaty soil, but some, especially the evergreens, are surprisingly tolerant. Trim off the old foliage of both sorts just as the new shoots start to grow in early spring.

Eryngium The sea hollies provide some of our best blues and often combine their round or spherical heads with blue-tinted or white-veined foliage. The names, unfortunately, are rather muddled. The richest blue is found in *E. × oliverianum*, 2 ft (60 cm). *E. planum* is taller and has much smaller flowers but far more of them and in a similar deep shade. Our native sea holly, *E. maritimum*, 12 in (30 cm), has broad grey leaves and pale blue flowers, while *E. bourgatii*, 2 ft (60 cm), has the best foliage, deeply cut and white-veined but with grey-green flowers. The eryngiums are an altogether tolerant group for almost any soil that is not waterlogged, although they do prefer full sun. Sea holly is best in very well-drained soil.

Euphorbia An increasingly popular group, the evergreens are almost shrubby and provide indispensable winter foliage and spring flowers. Many of the truly herbaceous ones are at their best rather later. There are now quite a few kinds of the evergreen *E. characias*, 2–4 ft (60 cm–1.2 m), available. All make upright stems

Epimedium × rubrum is a useful plant for a shady spot. Although grown primarily for its foliage, it has dainty pink flowers in spring

lined with narrow, sometimes blue-tinted foliage, topped with cylindrical heads of greeny yellow flowers, dark-eyed except in sub-species *wulfenii*. 'Lambrook Gold' (see p. 36) is especially impressive. All are good and grow in a variety of positions but are at their best in hot, dry sites where they will probably self-sow. Similar in habit is *E. rigida*, 18 in (45 cm), with stunning silvery blue foliage and yellow flower heads, but this demands sun and good drainage. A little later comes the truly herbaceous *E. polychroma* with brilliant acid-yellow flowers, an easy and tolerant plant, though best in the sun. Later still is *E. sikkimensis*, 4 ft (1.2 m), which runs at the root. It starts the year with red shoots pushing through the soil, develops white-veined leaves along its stems and tops them with greenish yellow flowers in early summer. Unlike many, it prefers a damp soil and will stand partial shade.

Gentiana Most gentians are alpines but a couple are fine perennials. The willow gentian, *G. asclepiadea*, 3 ft (90 cm), needs woodland conditions and its arching branches are lined with pairs of sparkling blue flowers. You would hardly know *G. lutea* as a gentian; 4 ft (1.2 m) high, upright, with clusters of yellow flowers at the leaf joints, it needs rich but not wet soil and full sun.

Geranium The cranesbills are immensely popular and come in a huge, and still increasing, range of species, hybrids and cultivars. I can only include a small selection. *G. endressii* and its hybrids make low, dense, weed-suppressing cover and flower for many weeks. 'Wargrave Pink' is an especially bright colour, 'Claridge Druce' is vigorous with slighly greyish foliage. 'Russell Prichard' flowers from June to October and spreads widely from a central rootstock. For further back in the border the summer-flowering *G. pratense*, 2 ft (60 cm), comes with single and double flowers in various blues and white. 'Plenum Violaceum' is a neat double, 'Galactic' is fine pure white. Those who like black flowers always look out for *G. phaeum*, 2 ft (60 cm), with its dainty reflexed blooms, but it varies from deepest maroon to lilac and even white. My favourite is *G. renardii*, 12 in (30 cm) (see p. 27). Not a typical cranesbill, its soft foliage has the texture and colour of sage leaves and sets off the white, purple-veined flowers beautifully. It makes a dense, rounded mound and needs a sunny spot at the front of the border where you can admire its markings. At its best a little earlier than most, *G. sylvaticum*, 3 ft (90 cm), is lovely in dappled shade. Naturally violet-blue in colour, 'Mayflower' is especially richly coloured with a white eye. Finally, *G. × magnificum*, 2 ft (60 cm), whose floppiness irritates some gardeners but whose rich, purplish blue, dark-veined flowers and long season win over so many more.

Geum The low, rough foliage may be undistinguished but the open sprays of flowers are delightful. Two seed-raised doubles, 2 ft (60 cm), the fiery red 'Mrs Bradshaw' and the yellow 'Lady Stratheden', are floriferous but their strong shades need careful placing. 'Borisii' is shorter and a warmer orange shade. All thrive in any reasonable soil in sun or partial shade.

Helenium These valuable summer- and autumn-flowering perennials are tough plants, producing a good show even in poor conditions. But they repay better soil, regular division and thoughtful support with sheets of flowers in yellow, rusty, coppery and chestnut shades. They range from the 2 ft (60 cm) orange-flowered 'Wyndley' to the 5 ft (1.5 m) orangey brown 'Moerheim Beauty'.

Helleborus Good hellebores are much sought after. Forget the cultivars propagated by division, which are almost impossible to find, expensive and not necessarily what they say they are. Modern selections are better and are offered more regularly. The *H. orientalis* hybrids, 18 in (45 cm), are the most captivating but also the most variable. Surprisingly tolerant garden plants, they are at their best in rich, limy soil in dappled shade. Modern selections are your best choice and you can now choose from white, various pinks, reds and purples, slaty blues, pure greens and primrose yellows – all with or without spots. These selections also have much better

Above: hellebores and pulmonaria, an effective combination of shade-tolerant perennials which flower in spring
Opposite: yellow *Kniphofia* 'Little Maid' is a useful accent plant and softer in colour than the more familiar red hot pokers (see p. 54)

shaped flowers than most old cultivars. The Christmas rose, H. niger, 12 in (30 cm), rarely flowers in December and is unhappy in some soils; but if your soil is well drained yet rich you should be able to grow it. The large-flowered 'Potter's Wheel' and the smaller but more floriferous 'White Magic' are impressive improvements on unselected seedlings. Two species with tall stems are easy to grow. H. argutifolius, 3 ft (90 cm), with apple green flowers and jagged foliage is best in the sun. The stinking hellebore, H. foetidus, 2 ft (60 cm), with small green cups edged in red, thrives in shade; 'Wester Flisk' is an impressive red-stemmed form. Hellebores are best left undivided for up to ten years to grow into imposing clumps, then divided in late summer.

Hemerocallis Day lilies compensate for opening each flower only for a day by producing them in a long succession. Modern hybrids have greatly extended the flowering period, reduced the height and improved the colour range. Many are scented. They are also tough, although they may need a favoured position and good drainage in the very coldest areas. 'Stella d'Oro', 18 in (45 cm), is one of the newer, shorter cultivars with slightly peachy yellow flowers. The even newer 'Pardon Me' in deep red is equally dwarf, while 'Little Grapette', 12 in (30 cm), is deep purple. Among the taller ones 'Corky', 3 ft (90 cm), is pale yellow, 'Mallard', 3 ft (90 cm), is rich red and 'Varsity', 2½ ft (76 cm), is creamy peach with a maroon eye.

Heuchera Enjoying a revival with the introduction of new hybrids, heucheras, 2ft (60 cm), thrive in well-drained soil in full sun but often give a good display in shadier and damper conditions. Many have good foliage and the slender stems lined with flowers from May to July come in an increasing range of colours; they are good for cutting. 'Palace Purple' has rich purple-bronze foliage and cream flowers, 'Snowstorm' has white-splashed foliage and red flowers. 'Greenfinch' has green flowers while in a stronger colour there is 'Scintillation' in bright pink.

Hosta Ever popular and appearing in a continuing stream of new forms, hostas are superb ground-cover plants for sun or shade and remarkably tough. With their sumptuous foliage in a generous range of leaf colours and variegations – not forgetting their pale flowers – they are indispensable. The rich green Hosta lancifolia has fine narrow leaves overlapping like fish-scales; 'Royal Standard' is much more imposing. 'Thomas Hogg' and the slightly more stylish 'Shade Fanfare' have good white-edged foliage. H. fortunei 'Aureo-marginata' and the rather smaller 'Golden Tiara' are yellow edged. H. fortunei 'Aurea', the neater growing 'Golden Prayers' and the very large and slug resistant 'Sum and Substance'

Lobelia 'Queen Victoria' is a bold plant which prefers a moist well-drained situation (see p. 54)

are all-gold. Of the blues, *H. sieboldiana* 'Bressingham Blue' is tall with puckered foliage. 'Krossa Regal' is even larger, 'Halcyon' is the best of the smaller blues while the ever popular 'Frances Williams' (see p. 15) has yellow-edged blue leaves. For flowers, 'Honeybells', 'Royal Standard', 'Sugar and Cream', 'Sum and Substance' and *H. tardiflora* are among the best. Hostas are best left undisturbed to grow into fat clumps. In a rich soil and partial shade, they need only protection from slugs and snails and a regular mulch to keep them happy.

Iris Irises are essential border plants and although the flowers all have the same general appearance they come in many colours. Flag or bearded irises are the traditional cottage-garden iris. Those flowering in April and May are shorter than the many June-flowering cultivars. The dwarf types, 12–24 in (30–60 cm), are ideal for small borders and gravel gardens. The June flags, 4 ft (1.2 m), are splendid border plants whose foliage is valuable after their relatively fleeting flowering season. Recommending cultivars is impossible – there are so many and they come in such an extraordinary range of shades, including maroons and yellows, that no one could be disappointed. They all like a sunny spot in almost any reasonably well-drained soil and are best divided and replaced every three or four years immediately after flowering. *Iris sibirica*, 3 ft (90 cm), is altogether different, with narrow upright foliage and a taste for damp soil. Its colours are restricted to blues, purples and white. The soft blue 'Papillon' is worth looking out for. These are best divided in early spring. For the hottest, driest spots *I. unguicularis*, 2 ft (60 cm), is essential and is at its happiest at the foot of a south facing wall. Sometimes starting to flower as early as November and continuing to April, its scented flowers appear among grassy foliage but need protection from slugs. *I. foetidissima* 2 ft (60 cm) (see p. 10), is a splendid plant for dry shade but thrives more heartily in better conditions. The deep green evergreen foliage is striking, its pretty flowers may be small but its sparkling orange-red berries are carried on arching shoots all winter. They usually self-sow.

Kniphofia Red hot pokers are no longer restricted to red and one of the most sought after is now 'Little Maid', 18 in (45 cm) (see p. 51), in ivory cream with green buds. 'Bressingham Comet' is a deep orange and even shorter. If you like tall traditional types, go all the way with the fiery red 'Prince Igor', 6 ft (1.8 m). Kniphofias are happiest in well-drained soil in full sun and are best divided in spring rather than autumn. They may need protection from frost and winter wet in more northerly areas.

Lobelia Perennial lobelias have a reputation for lack of hardiness but slugs and rots seem more of a problem than frost. Their upright growth and richly coloured flowers, coupled in some cases with beetroot red foliage, make them invaluable for borders which are not too dry. 'Queen Victoria' (see p. 53), with red flowers and very dark red foliage is one of the best. Even more widely grown is *L. cardinalis*, with green foliage and red flowers. Of the more modern cultivars, 'Dark Crusader' is rich red, 'Compliment Scarlet' is pillar-box red while 'Russian Princess' has purple flowers and dark foliage.

Lupinus Easy to grow, colourful and flamboyant as cut flowers, it is obvious why lupins are so popular. Best on acid soils, most are now raised from seed and many will flower in the first year from an early sowing. 'Dwarf Gallery', 2 ft (60 cm), is very prolific in a good selection of colours while 'New Generation', 4 ft (1.2 m), is tall and ele-

Lychnis coronaria 'Oculata' forms an upright silvery clump and is ideal for planting in a sunny position (see p. 56)

Although peonies are not easy to propagate, their flowers and foliage are well worth having in any border. This example is *Paeonia mlokosewitschii*

gant with a bonus of retaining its lowest flowers until the top most ones are open. The colour range is wonderful but they will need staking as the spikes are so long and heavy.

Lychnis Rather a mixed bunch but all are happy in sun and any reasonable soil. They are also good for cutting. 'Dusty Miller', *L. coronaria*, 2–3 ft (60–90 cm), is easily raised from seed and will self-sow generously when happy. It thrives on a dry soil and the grey felted leaves show off the magenta flowers well. The white form and 'Oculata' (see p. 55), a pink-eyed white, are especially effective. Taller and more stiffly upright is the brilliant red *L. chalcedonica*, 3–4 ft (90 cm–1.2 m), with flat heads of small flowers; there are also examples with less attractive pink, white and double flowers.

Meconopsis Most meconopsis are better in the north and west than the drier south and east. But they are worth giving the humus-rich, acid soil and shelter from icy winds that they like for the sake the almost unbelievable blue flowers. The Welsh poppy, *M. cambrica*, 15 in (38 cm), is the exception and will grow almost anywhere, its pale ferny-like foliage setting off the delicate yellow or orange flowers well. It can self-sow too much when happy. Of the blue poppies, *M. betonicifolia*, 3ft (90 cm), is the easiest to grow, is a good perennial when happy and is easily raised from seed. It is best divided every three or four years in September.

Monarda Bee balm or bergamot is a fine border plant, with aromatic foliage and flowers carried in tiers up the stem. It creeps well if given sunshine and moist soil though it should not be waterlogged in winter. In dry summers mildew can be a problem. Most of those available are hybrids and the brighter red 'Cambridge Scarlet', the deep purple 'Prairie Night' and the pure white 'Snowmaiden' are all good. There is also a range of mildew-resistant cultivars named after the signs of the zodiac.

Paeonia The flowers of peonies may be fleeting but they are captivating while at their best. Some gardeners prefer the simplicity of the species, others the opulence of the double hybrids. Most are happy in a rich but well-drained soil and are best left undisturbed until they show signs of deteriorating. The so-called Molly-the-witch, *P. mlokosewitschii*, 2ft (60 cm) (opposite), not only flowers early but its lemony flowers are a lovely pure shade. There is an ever expanding range of hybrids, 3 ft (90 cm), many from America, and all have the benefit of good foliage to follow the large flowers which may be single, fully double or with a mass of shorter petals in the centre. It is impossible to make a selection; I can only advise choosing from a Chelsea Flower Show display or a well-labelled garden and obtaining those that particularly catch your fancy.

Papaver Oriental poppies, 2–3 ft (60–90 cm), are nothing if not colourful, and thrive in sunshine and well-drained soil, preferably one which is not over-rich. The leaves disappear in early summer leaving an awkward gap which must be masked by a late developer. The roots go deep and are apt to re-shoot if a plant is moved. 'Black and White' (see p. 1), has pure white flowers with a black blotch at the base of each petal. 'Mrs Perry' is a salmony pink, 'Turkish Delight' is soft pink. For more fiery shades, go for the scarlet 'Goliath'.

Phlox Border phlox like sun for most or all of the day and a rich soil that is not too dry. Their fragrance is powerful, although not everyone can smell it. The two groups are based on *P. maculata* and *P. paniculata*. The former has cylindrical flower heads made up of myriads of small flowers and is well scented. The lilac-pink 'Alpha', and 'Omega' in white with a lilac eye, are the most often seen although the pure white 'Miss Lingard' is well worth seeking out. Most cultivars derive from *P. paniculata*, and there are many. As with poppies, I recommend choosing on the basis of plants in flower, but I suggest you look out for the deep lilac 'Branklyn', 2ft (60 cm), and the dark-eyed pink 'Eva Callum', 3ft (90 cm), which are shorter than most. There are also examples with variegated foliage; 'Nora Leigh' (see p. 58) has white-edged leaves and 'Harlequin' is variegated in white and pink. The cultivars of *P. paniculata*, in par-

(1.5 m), is a lovely gentian blue although it may need support, and there is the sparkling azure S. *uliginosa*, 5 ft (1.5 m), with rather sparse, waving stems. A covering of leaf litter is useful in winter.
Sedum The autumn-flowering S. *spectabile* and its hybrids, 18 in (45 cm), are mong the finest of late summer and autumn flowers and are much loved by butterflies. The flat flower heads are set off by succulent bluish foliage. They thrive in sunshine and good soil and can easily be increased by spring cuttings. 'Autumn Joy' has grey-blue leaves and is one of the later ones, with large pink heads eventually turning coppery. 'September Glow' is darker in flower and 'Iceberg' is white. 'Vera Jameson', 9 in (23 cm) (below), has pale pink flowers but strongly purple-tinted foliage. 'Ruby Glow', 9 in (23 cm) (below), is daintier, with small heads of pink flowers.
Symphytum Some comfreys can be very invasive; all are tough, thriving in shade and less than perfect soil. 'Hidcote Blue' and 'Hidcote Pink', both 2ft (60 cm), are fine ground coverers but their spreading habits may be inconvenient. Equally spreading but half the height is the creamy-flowered S. *ibericum* (syn. S. *grandiflorum*), 12 in (30 cm), with dark green leaves. The yellow-margined 'Goldsmith' is said to be a variegated form of this species but has pale blue flowers. More like a hosta at first, S. × *uplandicum* 'Variegatum' has long, oval greyish-green leaves margined in cream with tall stems of pinkish-lilac flowers. A lovely plant.

The succulent foliage of the late-flowering sedums, such as S. 'Ruby Glow', looks good long before the richly-coloured flowers open

Short lists of perennials with different qualities and for difficult situations. For more information on those not already described in this handbook, refer to the books listed in the bibliography on p. 64.

Acid soil
Epimedium
Gentian
Lupinus
Meconopsis
Trillium

Clay soil
Anemone × hybrida
Bergenia
Hellebore
Inula
Rodgersia

Climbers
Dicentra macrocapnos
Eccremocarpus scaber
Humulus lupulus 'Aureus'
Lathyrus
Tropaeolum speciosum

Damp shade
Ferns
Hellebore
Hosta
Polygonatum
Tricyrtis

Dry shade
Alchemilla mollis
Carex pendula
Iris foetidissima
Polystichum setifeum
Periwinkles (Vinca)

Hot and dry sites
Euphorbia characias
Zauschneria
Acanthus spinosus
Crambe maritima
Eryngium maritimum

Late flowering
Aster lateriflorus 'Horizontalis'
Helenium
Dendranthemum
 (Chrysanthemum)
 'Anastasia', 'Bronze
 Elegance'
Liriope spicata
Salvia uliginosa

Quick spreaders
Achillea millifolium hybrids
Achillea ptarmica
Anemone × hybrida
Lamium maculatum
Polygonum bistorta

Scented flowers
Lily of the valley (Convallaria)
Pinks and border carnations
 (Dianthus)
Hesperis
Oenotheras
Phlox

Seaside gardens
Alstroemeria
Crocosmia
Iris
Kniphofia
Sedum

Shallow, limy soil
Pulsatilla
Periwinkle (Vinca)
Euphorbia robbiae
Lamium
Primula veris

Waterlogged soil
Astilbe
Caltha
Ligularia
Lysichitum
Primula (candelabra types)

Blue leaves
Hosta 'Halcyon'
Elymus magellanicus
Parahebe perfoliata
Festuca
Euphorbia rigida

Bronze leaves
Acaena 'Copper Carpet'
Carex comans 'Bronze Form'
Crocosmia 'Solfaterre'
Rumex flexuosus
Euphorbia griffithii 'Dixter'

Grey leaves
Anaphalis
Artemisia
Dianthus
Lychnis coronaria
Stachys byzantina

Purple leaves
Heuchera 'Palace Purple'
Cimicifuga racemosa 'Brunette'
Euphorbia amygdaloides
 'Rubra'
Foeniculum vulgare 'Smoky'
Sedum 'Vera Jameson'

Variegated leaves
Hosta 'Thomas Hogg'
Astrantia 'Sunningdale
 Variegated'
Ajuga reptans 'Variegata'
Iris foetidissima 'Variegata'
Mentha suaveolens 'Variegata'

Yellow leaves
Carex stricta 'Aurea'
Hosta fortunei 'Aurea', 'Sum
 and Substance'
Lysimachia nummularia
 'Aurea'
Melissa officinalis 'All Gold'
Tanacetum parthenium
 'Aureum'

Further Information

SPECIALIST SOCIETIES

The Hardy Plant Society is the only society devoted exclusively to hardy perennials. It issues two well-illustrated bulletins and three newsletters annually, and organises a seed exchange. There are local groups all over the country which organise regular garden visits, plant sales, talks and study days and publish their own newsletters. For details of membership contact the Administrator, Hardy Plant Society, Bank Cottage, Great Comberton, Pershore, Worcestershire WR10 3DP.

The Cottage Garden Society also has an interest in hardy perennials. It produces regular newsletters, organises events and runs a seed exchange. For details of membership contact The Secretary, Cottage Garden Society, 5 Nixon Close, Thornhill, Dewsbury, West Yorkshire WF12 0JA.

The Alpine Garden Society covers many of the smaller hardy perennials as well as alpines. For membership details contact The Secretary, Alpine Garden Society, Avon Bank, Pershore, Worcestershire WR10 3JP.

NURSERIES

There are a large number of nurseries which sell a good range of hardy perennials; some are general nurseries, some are specialists. I have bought plants from the following nurseries and can recommend them. I suggest that you check in *The Plant Finder* for the availability of individual plants, up-to-date opening times and catalogue prices. Not all nurseries run a mail order service, and not all are open to callers.

Axeltree Nursery, Starvecrow Lane, Peasmarsh, Rye, East Sussex TN31 6XL.
Blackthorn Nursery, Kilmeston, Alresford, Hampshire SO24 0NL.
Bressingham Gardens, Bressingham, Diss, Norfolk IP22 2AB.
Four Seasons Nursery, Forncett St Mary, Norwich, Norfolk NR16 1JT.

Glebe Cottage Plants, Pixie Lane, Warkleigh, Umberleigh, North Devon EX37 9DH.
Goldbrook Plants, Foxne, Eye, Suffolk IP21 5AN.
Holden Clough Nursery, Holden, Bolton-by-Bowland, Clitheroe, Lancashire, BB7 4PF.
Hopleys Plants, High Street, Much Hadham, Herts SG10 6BU.
Margery Fish Plant Centre, East Lambrook Manor, East Lambrook, South Petherton, Somerset TA13 5HL.
Monksilver Nursery, Oakington Road, Cottenham, Cambridge CB4 4TW.
Stillingfleet Lodge Nurseries, Stillingfleet, Yorkshire, YO4 6HW.
Unusual Plants, Beth Chatto Gardens, Elmstead Market, Colchester CO7 7DB.
Washfield Nursery, Horns Road, Hawkhurst, Kent TN18 4QU.

RECOMMENDED READING

Alan Bloom's Hardy Perennials by Alan Bloom (Christopher Helm)
Garden Flowers from Seed by Christopher Lloyd & Graham Rice (Viking)
The Green Tapestry by Beth Chatto (Collins)
Hardy Perennials by Roger Phillips & Martyn Rix (Pan)
Hardy Plants and Alpines by Alan Bloom (Floraprint)
Perennial Garden Plants by Graham Stuart Thomas (Dent)
The Plant Finder edited by Chris Philip and Tony Lord, (published annually in association with the Hardy Plant Society and distributed by Moorland Publishing)
Plantsmen on Plants edited by Richard Bird (Hardy Plant Society)

There are a number of Wisley Handbooks which are of particular interest to enthusiasts for hardy perennials. These include

Delphiniums, Foliage Plants, The Mixed Border, Primroses and Auriculas.

Other books by Christopher Lloyd, Margery Fish and Beth Chatto also contain plenty of information on hardy perennials.